If it makes me better, why should I stop?

"Just leave me alone" or "What I need now is chocolate!" We've all said it, and most of the time it's not a problem at all.

But when you're feeling down, the things that get you through can also become the things that mess you up.

Being alone ends up isolating us. One bar of chocolate becomes a comfort eating habit. One drink becomes a whole bottle. One scratch becomes a cycle of risky self-harm. One question "Are you still my friend?" becomes a constant need for reassurance.

And instead of getting better, you get worse.

But this doesn't need to happen! Turn the page and you'll be taking the first step towards getting in control of the things you do.

YOU'RE ON YOUR WAY!

The first step is the most important

And you just took it. You made the decision to stop letting unhelpful behaviours mess up your life.

Now, we're going to help you work out what you're doing too much of, and then show you a simple 4-step way to stop or cut down.

How do you know when something is messing you up?

Turn over

IT AIN'T WHAT YOU DO, IT'S HOW MUCH YOU DO IT

We're not here to be killjoys. There's nothing wrong with chocolate, spending some time alone, or a bit of retail therapy.

But when you're feeling low, you can start to lean on these things, using them to help get you through a bad time.

Other, not so obvious behaviours can also be 'props'. Like hitting out at people – physically or by shouting. Hurting yourself in different ways. Hiding away from the world.

Trouble is, too much of this kind of stuff makes you worse, not better. You get into a kind of vicious circle, doing something that seems to help for a bit, but finding that it actually makes life worse in the long run.

Are you doing too much of something?

Drinking	2 or 3 drinks a week	More than 2 or 3 a week but not getting drunk
Eating for comfort	Eating chocolate etc. occasionally	Eating a little when you feel upset
Spending Too Much	Buying some things you just fancy	Buying some things that stretch you financially
Taking risks	Seeing occasional risks as fun	You start to "up the stakes" to more dangerous risks
Complaining	You say clearly what you feel and need	You moan a lot that "It's not fair"
Being clingy	You lack some confidence at times	You want others to make important decisions for you
Hitting out at people	You're sometimes rude when frustrated	You begin to throw your weight around
Gossiping	You tell others good news about your friends	You discuss good news told in confidence
Shoplifting	Your friends say they shoplift and you don't tell them it's wrong	You're with friends when they steal and don't say anything
Hiding away	You tend to be quiet in conversations	You avoid spending time with people

A drink every day, sometimes getting drunk	Getting really drunk when you're down	Getting drunk every day
Eating a lot when you feel upset	Bingeing on food when you're upset	Bingeing and making yourself sick when you're upset
Getting into debt – but under control	Spending far more than comes in each week – ignoring the consequences	Run out of credit, paralysed and overwhelmed by debt
You start to get minor injuries	You do things that would put you in hospital if they went wrong	You do things that could be fatal for you or others
You get really upset if you don't get your own way	You get really worked up and upset others too	You are so upset you don't get on with other things and fall out with everyone
You ask other people's opinions all the time	You need others to be near you to feel okay	Your confidence is shot - you can't face anything alone
You often hurt people you don't like	You hit out at people you love when you feel frustrated	You get into fights often - hurting people and being injured yourself
You love to discuss people's private secrets	You get a reputation as someone who can't be trusted	No-one trusts you and you feel lonely
You take something small and say "it's no big deal"	You steal bigger and bigger things more and more often	Your shop-lifting continues and you start to steal in other ways too
You cross the road to avoid chats with people you know	You lose confidence and find it hard even knowing where to start a conversation	You stay in all the time feeling anxious, panicky and depressed

Want to stop or cut down? **Turn over!**

OK.
SO YOU
NEED TO
WORK ON
SOMETHING

Here's how...

First, don't beat yourself up. Most people get into a cycle of doing unhelpful things when they're feeling down. It's bad for you, and often for other people too.

The fact that you're reading this means you're on the way to fixing it.

All you have to do is choose one problem behaviour to work on, and follow our Easy 4-Step Plan (E4SP for short) to get control.

First choose a problem

The Things You Do

Are you:

Are you eating too many sweet things?

Tick ☐

Sitting around all day?

Tick ☐

Spending too much or little?

Tick ☐

Are you taking any tablets as prescribed?

Tick ☐

Keeping worries to yourself?

Tick ☐

Looking to others for help all the time?

Tick ☐

Lashing out at people?

Tick ☐

Trusting people you don't really know?

Tick ☐

Are you overdoing the phone calls?

Tick ☐

Hiding away?

Tick ☐

That Mess You Up

linked
worksheet
www.llttf.com

Being impulsive about important things?

Tick

Setting yourself up to fail/be rejected?

Tick

Becoming a TV/Internet addict?

Tick

Wanting others to sort out every problem?

Tick

Doing, doing, doing?

Tick

Drinking too much alcohol/coffee/cola to pick yourself up?

Tick

Sleeping in the whole day?

Tick

Putting things off?

Tick

Worrying all the time?

Tick

Other: please write any other things you do that mess you up here

This way to something good

13

NOW CHOOSE SOMETHING TO DO THAT HELPS

Choose a sensible response

Just one tiny change to what you do and how you react can make all the difference.

Like what?

Well, how about planning and preparing for a good night's sleep. Or why not try doing something that gives you a boost, such as a hobby, having a relaxing bath, or listening to music? Pick something that you think you might feel motivated to do, and of course something that you think you could keep working at.

There are many helpful things that you could do. Choose one or more that you might do instead of the things you do that mess you up.

Helpful things checklist ahead!

The Things You Do

Are you:

Eating regularly and healthily?

Tick ☐

Giving yourself time to sleep?

Tick ☐

Keeping up with routine things like keeping up with the house?

Tick ☐

Doing things with other people?

Tick ☐

Doing things that cheer you up?

Tick ☐

Sharing problems with trusted friends and family?

Tick ☐

Finding out more about how you feel?

Tick ☐

Letting upsetting thoughts just be?

Tick ☐

That Help

linked
worksheet
www.llttf.com

Facing your fears?

Tick ☐

Doing exercise/going for walks/
swimming etc?

Tick ☐

Using your sense of humour to
cope?

Tick ☐

Planning time for you as well as
for others?

Tick ☐

Regularly taking the medicine
prescribed by your doctor?

Tick ☐

Relaxing - with music, a film, a
book or whatever works for you?

Tick ☐

Asking for help from people
around you?

Tick ☐

Doing the essentials like
paying bills?

Tick ☐

Q: Am I doing other things that help?
Write in what you are doing if this
applies to you?

Now, use the Easy 4 Step plan to
make changes.

E4SP this way  17

Break the problem into pieces

It's hard to stop doing something all at once, especially if you've been doing it for ages, so break it into easy chunks.

So, if you've lost your confidence and are hiding away from the world, what could you do? You could break the week into bits and decide to do something with someone else on Mondays, for example.

Don't try and become a party animal yet - just work on a little bit of the problem - like getting out of the house.

Or if you're spending too much, start by just cutting out online shopping.

Most problems can be chopped up like this, and you're much more likely to succeed when you do things bit by bit.

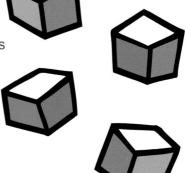

Brainstorm ways to do the first piece

Grab a piece of paper and write down all the things you could do to work on the first bit of the problem.

To meet up with somebody on Mondays, for example, you could ask a friend round, meet one or more people somewhere quiet and comfortable, or try something small like an email, phone call or text. Do anything that reconnects you to others and moves things on.

The trick is to be creative and let your mind go. Write everything down - the ridiculous things as well as the sensible ones.

Do this and there's bound to be a good idea in there somewhere.

TURN OVER FOR STEPS 3 & 4

Phone or text a friend

meet just one person

meet a few

Choose an idea and make a plan to do it

Look at your list of ideas and pick one that looks do-able. Remember, to make a big change in your life you are best chunking this into a series of smaller pieces. Make sure that the steps are small, straightforward and seem like things you could really do.

Choose something that is:

- Useful for understanding or changing how you are.
- Specific, so that you will know when you have done it.
- Realistic, practical and achievable.

Make each step as small as you like.

Now plan out what you'll do and when.

- *What* are you going to do?
- *When* are you going to do it?

Make sure your plan doesn't push you too far or too fast. Make it slow and easy to do so you move forward step by step.

Going to meet on Monday? You need to get it sorted a day or so before. On the Saturday, text your friend and ask them round on Monday evening. Ask them to let you know if they can make it, or whether another time is better.

What if something gets in the way?

As soon as you've written your plan, think about what could stop it happening. Is there anything that might trip you up?

- What could arise, and how can you overcome any problems?

When you know what could block your progress, make a mini-plan for getting round the block. This way, you'll be ready for whatever happens!

Check the plan and put it into action

This is it! You've made your plan, now you need to check that it's do-able. Use this checklist:

Is it realistic?
You're not planning to run a marathon are you?

Are you aiming at just one thing?
Don't try and do more than one item on your list. You can always pick another when you've sorted out the first one.

Is it slow?
There's no need to rush at things. Your plan can take as long as you like, so long as you stick to it, step by step.

Is it easy?
Make your steps small and easy and you'll be more likely to do them.

Are you ready to unblock it?
Have you thought about what could go wrong and how to deal with it?

FIVE TICKS?

THEN GO FOR IT!

NOW
KEEP
IT
GOING!

Just take it step by step

Even a problem that seems huge can be tackled with the E4SP. The secret is breaking everything down into small, manageable pieces.

When you're making your plan, be sure that the steps are small and do-able. Plan to cut down unhelpful behaviours and replace them with helpful one's.

When you're doing your plan, take it step by step and if things get scary in the middle, give yourself a rest or a breather. If it seems too much- take a step back and do something a bit easier for a time.

Then get back on track, until you've put your plan into action.

Be steady and determined, use the E4SP and you will be able to stop doing the things that mess you up, and build more helpful responses.

Use the Planner sheet on pages 24/25 to help you plan these changes.

Good Luck!

Make a plan!
Planner Sheet

1. What am I going to do?

2. When am I going to do it?

3. What problems or difficulties could arise, and how can I overcome them?

Is my planned task -

Q. Useful for understanding or
   changing how I am?

Yes	No
☐	☐

Q. Specific, so that I will
   know when I have done it?

Yes	No
☐	☐

Q. Realistic, practical
   and achievable?

Yes	No
☐	☐

WHERE TO GET EVEN MORE HELP

The E4SP works really well and if you need more details on using the E4SP (plus a lot more examples) get hold of 'How to Fix Almost Everything' - another booklet in this series.

But if you've tried the plan and come up against something you just can't seem to plan your way out of, you may need a bit more help than this little book can give. You can get added help and support by working through the free linked online modules at www.llttf.com.

When you've sorted your current problem, you might want to choose another little book and work on something else in your life. Here are some more little books that can help you deal with these things and start to feel better.

GOOD LUCK!